AN IDEAS INTO A......

Communicating Across Cultures

IDEAS INTO ACTION GUIDEBOOKS

Aimed at managers and executives who are concerned with their own and others' development, each guidebook in this series gives specific advice on how to complete a developmental task or solve a leadership problem.

LEAD CONTRIBUTORS	Don W. Prince
	Michael H. Hoppe
CONTRIBUTORS	Meena S. Wilson
	Maxine A. Dalton
GUIDEBOOK ADVISORY GROUP	Victoria A. Guthrie
	Cynthia D. McCauley
	Russ S. Moxley
DIRECTOR OF PUBLICATIONS	Martin Wilcox
EDITOR	Peter Scisco
WRITER	Janet Fox
DESIGN AND LAYOUT	Joanne Ferguson
CONTRIBUTING ARTISTS	Laura J. Gibson
	Chris Wilson, 29 & Company

CCL No. 406
ISBN No. 1-882197-59-3

CENTER FOR CREATIVE LEADERSHIP
POST OFFICE BOX 26300
GREENSBORO, NORTH CAROLINA 27438-6300
336-288-7210
WWW.CCL.ORG / PUBLICATIONS

AN IDEAS INTO ACTION GUIDEBOOK

Communicating Across Cultures

Don W. Prince and Michael H. Hoppe

Center for Creative Leadership

NORTH AMERICA EUROPE ASIA

www.ccl.org

THE IDEAS INTO ACTION GUIDEBOOK SERIES

This series of guidebooks draws on the practical knowledge that the Center for Creative Leadership (CCL®) has generated in the course of more than thirty years of research and educational activity conducted in partnership with hundreds of thousands of managers and executives. Much of this knowledge is shared – in a way that is distinct from the typical university department, professional association, or consultancy. CCL is not simply a collection of individual experts, although the individual credentials of its staff are impressive; rather it is a community, with its members holding certain principles in common and working together to understand and generate practical responses to today's leadership and organizational challenges.

The purpose of the series is to provide managers with specific advice on how to complete a developmental task or solve a leadership challenge. In doing that, the series carries out CCL's mission to advance the understanding, practice, and development of leadership for the benefit of society worldwide. We think you will find the Ideas Into Action Guidebooks an important addition to your leadership toolkit.

Table of Contents

EXECUTIVE BRIEF

If you are a manager anywhere in the world, you are almost certainly dealing with people of nationalities and cultures different from your own. In multinational business environments, communicating effectively with people who have languages, customs, and expectations different from yours is a necessary skill. If you are a manager anywhere in the world, you are almost certainly facing this kind of multicultural situation. This guidebook explains how to become aware of cultural differences, how to recognize when cultural differences pose a leadership challenge, and how to adapt your communication style to enhance your effectiveness as a manager.

When Being Yourself Isn't Enough

Many managers take it for granted that the way they greet colleagues, give direction to subordinates, present ideas to staff, and converse at business lunches is fine and appropriate. After all, skillful communication is a key tool that effective leaders work to master.

You might wonder then why you can't just keep speaking and writing as you always have, even if some of the people across the table, down the hall, or at the other end of the phone happen to come from countries and belong to nationalities other than your own. The answer to your question is that your natural, customary ways of communicating can have an unexpected and unwanted impact on people whose cultural backgrounds are different from yours. And you are just as likely to misunderstand and misinterpret their words and behavior.

Unless you make a conscious effort to be sensitive to different cultural styles, to recognize signals of culture clash, and to modify your own communications accordingly, you risk at the very least confusion and embarrassment. More critically, cross-cultural communication blunders can lead to more serious consequences—lost confidence, lost customers, and lost business relationships and opportunities.

In our ever-more-connected world, cross-cultural awareness and ability is no longer just a polite gesture to your international customers and colleagues. It's a new essential for leading in a global environment. This guidebook can help you improve your skills in cross-cultural communications. From this guidebook you'll learn how to:

- Expect and identify cultural differences.
- Look out for cultural differences.
- Draw cues from nonverbal communication.
- Speak and write clearly for other cultures.
- Learn the importance of names and titles.
- Use humor judiciously.
- Show your respect for other cultures.
- Become a lifelong learner of other cultures.

Anticipate and Adapt to Cultural Differences

To communicate effectively across cultures, you need to be able to anticipate those differences so that you are prepared to bridge the cultural divide by adapting your communication style. Acquiring these skills means concentrating on four points. First, examine your own cultural conditioning. Second, review your experiences with other cultures. Third, watch for discomfort that can signal cultural differences. Fourth, recognize and modify your communication approach.

Examine Your Own Cultural Conditioning

The way you express yourself, or the way you show that you are pleased, grateful, or angry, for example, is determined by the culture in which you live. Further, cultural conditioning goes beyond language and expressions. It defines, among other things, the subjects you consider appropriate for discussion, your perception of time, the amount of privacy and personal space you need to feel comfortable, and the manner in which you address the people around you—your boss, your friends, your family, your peers, or the people working for you. Around the world, different cultures carry very different attitudes about fundamental things, and express those attitudes in diverse ways. Within each culture, these attitudes form a commonsensical approach to life. No single culture is more correct or less advantageous than any other—it's not a matter of a right way or a wrong way. Your way is one among many.

> *As leader of a task force, Cheryl is having difficulties managing Chen, one of the team members. He promised to compile a report by the deadline she set, but he didn't. When she talks to him about it, he won't look her in the eye. Cheryl suspects that Chen is either very disorganized or doesn't respect her as a leader. His unwillingness to make eye contact looks like evasive behavior to her.*

In Cheryl's culture, deadlines are firm commitments, and making eye contact is a sign of honesty. She knows that Chen is from a different culture, but she is not aware of how strongly her own culture has influenced her conclusions about his behavior.

Becoming aware of your own cultural conditioning requires you to step outside of your cultural borders. That's not an easy task, but here are five questions to ask yourself that can help you recognize the influence of your own cultural boundaries on your communication style.

1. Do I understand my own cultural background and conditioning?
2. Do I approach interpersonal encounters on the job with an awareness of how differences may affect communication?
3. Do I have the attitude that "different" is bad, inferior, or wrong?

4. Am I aware of ways that I stereotype others?

5. Am I willing to adjust my communication in order to be more effective?

Review Your Experiences with Other Cultures

You can also build your cultural awareness by reviewing your experiences with other cultures. All of us are from time to time likely to find ourselves in situations in which we are the cultural outsider. Perhaps you've attended a wedding, funeral, or holiday gathering that is completely unfamiliar to your understanding of such ceremonies. Perhaps you have traveled abroad and returned with anecdotes about the strange behavior and customs of the people you encountered.

In these casual brushes with other cultures, we may taste unfamiliar food, meet people who are either more or less emotionally expressive than we are, or find ourselves more crowded or with more personal space than we're comfortable with. The pace of conversation may seem faster or slower.

Here are three actions you can take to review your experiences with other cultures:

1. Make a list of lessons learned in previous cross-cultural interactions. What did you learn? How did you learn it?

2. Review your previous cross-cultural encounters. What communication difficulties did you experience? How did you overcome them?

3. Reflect on which cross-cultural differences are the most difficult for you to adjust to. Why do you think that is?

Watch for Discomfort that Can Signal Cultural Differences

During a visit to a foreign country, distant city, or even another company, cultural differences can seem colorful, exotic, and appealing. But when the time spent in another culture is longer than a visit—or when you work and conduct business with people of other cultures—your cultural biases can emerge with more force. The disregard for time that seemed so delightful on the island vacation feels very different on Monday morning in the office when the clock is ticking. A modest, deferential manner that was appealing in one cultural context may strike you as passive and ineffectual in a conference room.

These experiences feel unfamiliar because we are looking through the lens of our own cultural expectations. Unconsciously, we expect other people to think, feel, and act the way we do. When they don't conform to our expectations, we put our own interpretations on their behavior. But when you're working across cultures, interpretation often becomes misinterpretation. You run the risk of negatively judging the words and actions of people of other cultures, or incorrectly assigning motives to unfamiliar behavior because you're viewing an experience from the limited perspective of your own culture.

The discomfort you feel when cultural boundaries collide can be used to your benefit by alerting you to cultural differences. In your interactions with other people, be aware that cultural differences may be coming into play when you experience such feelings as confusion, anxiety, frustration, misunderstanding, tension, impatience, irritation, or anger.

When you feel uncomfortable, it's natural to retreat from that discomfort. After all, you probably feel you are most effective as a manager when you are operating from a familiar place, where you can draw confidence and make decisions based on past experience.

From our work at CCL, we have coined the phrase "jump-back response" to describe this desire to retreat. To be more effective when communicating across cultures, resist your jump-back response. Stay with the discomforting experience and learn from it. Compare the unexpected and discomforting behaviors you experience when communicating across cultures and compare them to your knowledge of your own cultural expectations.

Why doesn't she just say yes or no? *In one culture an indirect answer may signal indecisiveness, while in another culture it signals deference and respect.*

Why is he always staring at me like that? *In one culture staring can signal aggressiveness or intimidation, while in another culture direct eye contact shows attention and esteem.*

Why does he have to get right in my face whenever he talks to me? *In one culture the halo of personal space and privacy can be much smaller than it is in another culture.*

Why doesn't she tell me if she doesn't understand something? *In one culture asking questions is accepted as an effective tool for communications, while in other cultures questioning superiors may signal insolence.*

Why does he sit there smiling when I'm talking about his performance problems? *In one culture smiling during a discussion about performance problems may signal contempt and disinterest, while in another culture a smile may reflect sincerity and attention.*

Why does he make a joke out of everything? *In one culture a glib nature can signal a lack of confidence or seriousness, while in another culture it's a sign of deference.*

Recognize and Modify Your Communication Approach

When you work with people of other cultures, you must expect that differences will surface, recognize those cultural differences by the discomfort they produce, and anticipate that those differences will create a need for more thoughtful and deliberate communication. Don't assume that your own cultural customs are correct and superior to others or take the attitude that the other person has to change his or her ways. Be alert to the need to modify your communication style when

- Another person's behavior makes you uncomfortable.
- Another person's response or reaction seems inappropriate or confusing.
- You assume that you're right and the other person is wrong.
- You stereotype and denigrate another cultural group.
- You ignore or exclude someone because understanding, and making yourself understood, seems too difficult.

It's important that you make changes to your communication patterns after you recognize that those changes are necessary. A person from another culture is likely to be forgiving the first and second times you make a mistake, but if you persist you will appear ignorant, insensitive, dismissive, or disrespectful.

Consider, for example, the use of "why" questions as a way to get more information. In some cultures, such as that of the United States, it's completely acceptable to ask "Why did you do the job this way?" In other cultures, Japan's for example, the same question is considered rude as it puts the other person on the defensive. In this case you can change your communication behavior: "That's an interesting approach you took to the problem. Tell me a little more about it." This gives the other person a chance to share more information with you without risk. Other simple changes that you can make after recognizing different cultural behaviors include learning how to make the correct greeting (a handshake? a bow? a hug?), when to offer your business card (before or after the other person?), and when and how to question superiors.

Listen and Watch for Cultural Differences

When you listen to people who have the same cultural background and native language as you do, you can usually get the gist of their meaning without special effort. You can easily understand their words and "read" their body language and tone of voice. You can make assumptions that are valuable shortcuts to understanding.

When you listen to people from other cultures, your task is more difficult. You can't make the same assumptions. Effective cross-cultural communication requires an extra measure of awareness and attention. To focus on the other person's message, keep these six questions in mind each time you communicate across cultures:

1. What do I know about this person's culture?
2. Do I take the time to focus on a person from another culture so that I can understand where he or she is "coming from"?
3. Do I pay attention to a person's words and body language?
4. Do I listen for feelings and unvoiced questions?
5. Do I clarify and confirm what I have heard?
6. Do I check to make sure the other person has fully understood what I said?

Capture, Clarify, and Confirm

There are three practical rules to ensuring better cross-cultural communications.

1. *Capture.* To avoid misunderstandings, injured feelings, and confusion, focus fully on the conversation. Capture what is said and refer to your knowledge about other cultures to make meaning.
2. *Clarify.* If you aren't completely sure you've understood what the other person is saying, look for nonverbal cues to explain the message. Alternatively, you can ask a knowledgeable insider to check your understanding.
3. *Confirm.* To make sure the other person has understood you, give him or her an opportunity to paraphrase or clarify what you have said. You might want to write down your message or schedule a short follow-up conversation to repeat, in a different way, your original message.

Look for Nonverbal Communication

Whether you're talking to someone from within your own culture or to someone with a different cultural perspective, much of the message is relayed through nonverbal cues. When communicating across cultures, it's important not only to hear what the other person is saying but also to observe what that person's body language (facial expressions, hand gestures, eye contact, tone of voice) is saying.

Keep in mind, however, that like spoken language nonverbal expressions such as eye contact and body position have different meanings in different cultures. A clenched fist, a slouched posture, an open hand, or a smile can tell us how to understand a communication only if we have a cultural context for defining the body language.

Even silence can communicate. In some cultures remaining silent after another person has spoken shows respectful contemplation and consideration of that person's words. If your culture doesn't allow for such conversational pauses, resist filling these gaps with additional explanations and alternative wording.

Also remember that body language is a two-way medium—your own gestures and facial expressions can have unintended messages when you are communicating with someone from another culture. Although your words may say otherwise, your body can communicate boredom, defiance, persuasion, or condescension.

How can you interpret, or "hear" all of that body language if you're not familiar with the other culture? Keep your eyes open for patterns of behavior among various cultural groups. Ask a trusted person from the cultural group. Read up on the business customs of other cultures and pull information from the Internet (travel sites can be especially helpful in describing cultural customs).

Another good place to start is with a look at your own body language. Ask someone to videotape a presentation that you give at your organization, or observe yourself in a mirror. Ask yourself

- What do my nonverbal communications look like?
- How might I be perceived by someone with a different cultural background?
- Do I match the stereotype of people from my country?
- How can I check if I suspect that my body language is being misinterpreted by someone from another culture?

Unexpected Behavior Can Signal Cultural Differences

You might assume that body language is a universal language. But in reality body movements and facial expressions don't all speak the same language. If you experience unexpected behavior when you are trying to communicate in a cross-cultural setting, it's likely the other person's culture is different than yours and that you are unfamiliar with the cultural context behind the behavior.

A manager is conducting an annual performance review with one of his direct reports. He begins the session by discussing all the areas in which the employee's performance met or exceeded goals. The employee listens attentively with a serious and thoughtful expression. But when the manager begins to discuss weaknesses and problem areas, the employee starts smiling. The sterner the manager's tone, the broader the employee grins. The employee doesn't comment on anything the manager says or defend or explain. The manager becomes angry because he believes the employee is mocking him and treating the evaluation as a joke.

Sustained eye contact means respect and attentiveness in some cultures, but is a rude invasion of privacy in others. A gesture that denotes enthusiastic approval in some cultures is an insult in others. In this case the employee's smile was not a sign of mockery but an expression of deep embarrassment and shame. The manager's angry feelings toward the employee's behavior signal that there may be a miscommunication because of cultural differences.

Frank and Nick leave the office to go to lunch together. When they get into the elevator, Nick stands one foot away from Frank, although the elevator is otherwise empty. When Frank moves a couple of steps away, Nick moves closer to him so that they are almost touching.

Every culture has its own standards about how much personal space feels right and comfortable. From Frank's cultural perspective, physical closeness is an expression of intimacy and feels completely inappropriate in a business relationship. In Nick's cultural view, such closeness is natural behavior. Putting more distance between himself and Frank shows that they don't know or don't like each other.

John goes to the airport to meet Yuri's plane. The two men had talked several times on the phone but had only met once before. When Yuri spots John in the baggage area, he enthusiastically embraces him and kisses him on both cheeks. John feels uncomfortable and hopes that nobody he knows has witnessed this greeting.

Every culture has its own unwritten rules about touching. In John's culture the only acceptable touching in business relationships is a handshake. In Yuri's culture bear hugs and kisses are an acceptable and even expected form of greeting, no matter what the relationship is and regardless of gender.

When Hong Mei presents her proposal at the meeting, Vincent reacts strongly. He pounds on the table and questions her in a loud voice. When Hong Mei casts her eyes down in embarrassment, Vincent seems to get more excited. He leans across the table and jabs his hand toward her face.

Every culture has its own ideas about what kind of emotional expression is acceptable and right. In Hong Mei's culture emotional reserve and restraint are cherished and expected. In Vincent's culture feelings are freely expressed in loud voices, expansive gestures, grimaces, groans, and exclamations. Anything less conveys coldness and disengagement.

Susan travels to London for a meeting with Gillian and Philip. She wants to make a good impression and to indicate that she is happy to be working with them, so she nods and smiles at their comments and observations.

Even the most innocent gestures can be misconstrued. Susan thinks that her smiles and nods indicate attentiveness and express her happiness at being part of the team. Gillian and Philip come from a cultural background in which attentiveness and sincerity are marked by a reserved demeanor. Susan's behavior indicates to them that she is insincere, superficial, and unprofessional.

Just as spoken words can be misunderstood during a cross-cultural encounter, so too can nonverbal behavior be misconstrued. If a behavior upsets you beyond what seems appropriate, that's a good sign that cultures are colliding, not communicating. Ask questions to make sure that you understand the meaning of behavior that seems out of place.

Speaking and Writing Across Cultures

When talking with people whose native language is the same as yours, you can speak quickly and use idioms and slang without losing the meaning of your message. In fact, idioms and slang can highlight points you make. For someone from outside of your culture, who has learned your language in a formal setting such as a school or university, your conversational style can create confusion, misunderstanding, or complete bewilderment.

To enhance your cross-cultural communication effectiveness, build awareness of your speaking and writing styles. Pay attention to how you talk. Consider how your words might strike someone who isn't completely familiar with your language. Think about the medium: Are you writing a letter? chatting in the hallway? sending an e-mail or fax? leaving a voice mail? delivering a presentation? Each of these communication channels has its own challenges when messages travel across cultures.

Follow these ten guidelines to make yourself more understandable to people who are not completely familiar with your culture and language.

1. *Speak clearly and a little more slowly than you usually do.* This gives the other person time to translate and process your message.

2. *Use an even tone of voice.* The person you're speaking to may not speak your language like a native, but that's not a reflection on intelligence. There's no need to raise your voice or "talk down."

3. *Pronounce your words clearly and enunciate carefully.* It's much easier for the other person to understand "Have you had lunch?" than "Jeet yet?" Avoid sloppy expressions such as "Y'wanna go?" or "Gotta run."

4. *Use the simplest and most common words in most cases.* Someone outside your culture probably acquired his or her knowledge of your language by reading and study. Vocabulary from language textbooks isn't always the same as the language that is spoken in the street or even in the conference room. It's often helpful to state something a different way if the person doesn't understand rather than repeating the same words more slowly. For example, if "Can I pass you the rolls?" gets a blank look, you can rephrase and ask "Would you like some bread?"

5. *Avoid slang and colloquial expressions.* Americans may immediately recognize the meaning of "They went the whole nine

yards" or "He went ballistic." But to someone with a different cultural frame of reference, this kind of verbal shorthand and allusion to popular culture is at best mystifying and at worst insulting because it excludes them from the conversation.

6. *Use stories and analogies that are universally understood.* Anecdotes and comparisons are great aids to understanding in any language and in every culture. Concepts like success, challenge, teamwork, growth, customer service, and change, for example, are usually best communicated by telling stories and making analogies. The only caution is to avoid sports and military references, which may be unfamiliar or controversial to some.

7. *Use inclusive language and avoid terms and labels that may be offensive.* You may think it's innocuous to refer to the whole staff as "you guys" or to the Asian cultures as "Oriental." But many such labels strike different cultures differently. Insults are serious matters in many cultures and subcultures.

8. *Be aware of language uses in other cultures.* In some Asian cultures, for example, the word "no" is considered impolite. These cultures use body language to communicate indirectly a negative response. As another example, listen to this question: "Would you like to take on this assignment?" Some cultures would hear this message as a polite command, others would interpret it as a legitimate inquiry.

9. *Use simple language and complete thoughts when writing to a person from another culture.* Clear language, complete sentences, and standard (not colloquial) expressions make it easier for non-native speakers to understand your written messages. By using memos, e-mail, letters, faxes, and reports to reinforce your spoken communications you decrease the chances of being misunderstood, especially if the other person has less than a perfect grasp of your native language. Clearly written messages

give the other person more time to process the information you are sharing. E-mail is a special case because some cultures (both inside and outside of business environments) use it hurriedly and in a conversational way. Write your e-mail as clearly as you would any business correspondence.

10. *Pay special attention to language during phone calls and when leaving voice mail messages.* These faceless encounters present special pitfalls. In some cultures a high value is placed on face-to-face meetings. Heavy reliance on disembodied communication may be interpreted as a lack of respect. In phone conversations it is especially important to ask questions to verify that you have understood what the other person is saying and that what you have said is also understood. When leaving voice messages, match your tone of voice to your meaning and intent, and speak slowly and clearly so that your words aren't garbled when the other person plays back the message. If it is an urgent message, say so. If you need to be called back, say so.

What's in a Name

You can probably recall times when people have mispronounced your name or called you by the wrong name. Depending on the context (a newcomer at work, a hurried hello, a large industry show), your reaction might have ranged from mild irritation to deep offense.

Getting names right is extremely important in cross-cultural relationships because it communicates respect for the other person. Often it's difficult because the sounds and spellings of names outside of your cultural boundaries may be unfamiliar and hard to remember.

Professional and honorific titles are an important part of names in many cultures. Addressing someone as Mister, Senora, Doctor, Herr, Signor, and Professor, for example, is proper in all cases except when speaking to a close personal friend. The North American custom of jumping to a first-name basis immediately, in almost all relationships, is not widely duplicated in other cultures. On the contrary, going straight to the first name or using a nickname is likely to be perceived as an unwelcome presumption of intimacy or, at best, a sign of ignorance and arrogance.

Your business relationship with a person of another culture will start well if it begins with your effort to know his or her name. Here are five guidelines.

1. If necessary, ask the person to say his or her name more than once, until you can say it correctly. Don't convey any frustration with your difficulty in learning the name. Make it clear that it's important to you to get it right.
2. Ask the other person if he or she prefers to be called something different. Some people use a shortened version of their given name or a nickname, others dislike the practice.
3. Don't translate a name into the equivalent name in your language just because it's easier for you to pronounce. Nikolai won't necessarily enjoy your turning him into a Nick, and Graciela may not answer to Gracie. Renaming a person according to your own cultural norms can easily be construed as your thinking that your culture is superior.
4. Ask the other person to spell his or her name or to write it down if that will help you remember. It's often a good idea to write down a phonetic spelling of the name on the person's

business card or in your address file so you can check the pronunciation when you call or meet again.

5. Make sure you understand the order of names, which varies from culture to culture. In some Asian countries, but not all, the surname comes first. In Latin American cultures, the mother's maiden name is part of the surname.

Using Humor Appropriately

Humor can be an effective communications device, but it's a potential disaster when it crosses cultural lines. The punch line of a joke or story often relies on an inflection, a tone of voice, or a reference to a particular piece of cultural knowledge that is unknown outside of that sphere.

Even members of the same cultural group vary greatly on what strikes them as funny. Some people are amused by irony and parody, others enjoy slapstick and practical jokes. Good-natured ribbing about someone's gender, ethnic background, age, appearance, or occupation is tricky (and unwise) even in the most culturally homogenized situations—you can get a smile, a laugh, or a lawsuit. The safest object of your humor is yourself.

If you use humor as part of your communications style, keep these guidelines in mind when you cross the cultural divide.

• Never attempt ethnic or sexual humor.

• Avoid teasing. What seems good-natured fun to your cultural group may be confusing, embarrassing, or offensive to someone from another cultural group.

• Don't take yourself too seriously, but don't be so self-deprecating that others will question your self-respect.

• Watch for cultural cues that define circumstances when humor is acceptable and when it is not.

Communicate Respect for Other Cultures

It's impossible to understand all the communication nuances from all the world's cultures. Endless varieties across cultures, individual preferences, and constant change make that goal impossible. But in today's global business environment, ignorance is a feeble excuse. If you want to present yourself as a citizen of the world and to work effectively across cultural boundaries, you must be able to communicate respect for the customs, habits, and rituals of others —especially for the people who work with you. Some knowledge and understanding of cultures different from your own can help you show that respect. Here's how to get it.

• *Study the cultures of the people with whom you work.* Locate the country on a globe. Find out what languages are spoken there, what religions are practiced, what form of government is in effect. Learn about the country's history, its industries, and its leaders— past and present—in politics, business, religion, and the arts. The Internet is an excellent tool for this kind of research.

• *Keep up with current events.* Subscribe to one daily newspaper that does a good job reporting international news and read at least one weekly magazine that covers the world.

How to Be a Global Learner

• *Build personal networks*. Expand and deepen your circle of cross-cultural relationships. Seek out the people from other cultures that you see at work and in your community. Get to know these people on a personal level.

• *Read more deeply and widely about other cultures*. Don't skip news stories with foreign place names in the headlines. Read the fiction, poetry, biographies, and histories of other countries and cultures.

• *Travel more*. Take advantage of opportunities to travel abroad. While outside of your culture, observe the world around you through a broader cultural lens. If possible, take part in traditional celebrations to learn more about the meaning behind the customs and rituals you encounter.

• *Learn a new language*. It's difficult for adults to learn another language, but not impossible. Enroll in an introductory foreign language course at a local college or listen to a taped course during your daily commute. Get a colleague from outside your culture to teach you some conversational phrases in his or her native language.

• *Learn some phrases from the primary languages of your colleagues*. Your object isn't to become fluent in another language (unless you're working in a country in which your language is not dominant). People outside of your culture will recognize the effort you have put into learning how to say simple things like "Hello," "Thank you," "Goodbye" and "How are you?" in their own language. Even these simple phrases display interest and respect.

• *Ask the people you work with about their countries.* Once you show interest, most people will want to talk about their own customs and what those traditions mean to them. They'll want to discuss the differences they see between their culture and yours.

Expanding Horizons

Viewing the world—an increasingly connected world—through a single cultural lens is not a luxury that managers can afford to keep. Instead, an expanded cultural horizon is becoming ever more essential to effective leadership. Teams, work groups, communities, and organizations become more diverse every day. Adding new lenses to your cultural viewpoint not only increases your awareness of other cultures and your effectiveness in working with people from other cultures, but also develops your understanding of your own cultural conditioning.

The personal and leadership benefits of an expanded cultural horizon are great in number and powerful in effect. You can appreciate different ways, maybe better ways, of accomplishing goals. You will gain insight into your own behavior. You can discover "out of the box" ways to communicate clearly and effectively. You will become more comfortable in suspending your judgment, thereby fostering a more creative work environment.

Cultural differences arise in all levels of an organization and affect all leaders, from the project team to the executive suite. As you become more aware of these differences and more skilled at communicating across those cultures, you become a better manager and more effective leader.

Suggested Readings

Axtell, R. E. (1985). *Do's and taboos around the world*. Elmsford, NY: Benjamin.

Bosrock, M. M. (1995). *Put your best foot forward, Europe: A fearless guide to international communication and behavior*. St. Paul, MN: International Education Systems.

Bosrock, M. M. (1997). *Put your best foot forward, Asia: A fearless guide to international communication and behavior* (2nd ed.). St. Paul, MN: International Education Systems.

Dresser, N. (1996). *Multicultural manners: New rules of etiquette for a changing society*. New York: John Wiley & Sons.

Elashmawi, F., & Harris, P. R. (1993). *Multicultural management: New skills for global success*. Houston: Gulf.

Ferraro, G. P. (1998). *The cultural dimension of international business*. New York: Prentice Hall.

Gannon, M. J. (1994). *Understanding global cultures: Metaphorical journeys through 17 countries*. Thousand Oaks, CA: Sage.

Harris, P. R., & Moran, R. T. (1996). *Managing cultural differences*. Houston: Gulf.

Hill, R. (1994). *EuroManagers and martians: The business culture of Europe's trading nations*. Brussels, Belgium: Europublications, Europublic SA/NV.

Hofstede, G. (1991). *Cultures and organizations: Software of the mind*. New York: McGraw-Hill.

Kohls, L. R. (1996). *Survival kit for overseas living: For Americans planning to live and work abroad*. Yarmouth, ME: Intercultural Press.

Morrison, T., Conaway, W. A., & Borden, G. A. (1994). *Kiss, bow, or shake hands: How to do business in 60 countries*. Holbrook, MA: Adams Media.

Stewart, E. C., & Bennett, M. J. (1991). *American cultural patterns: A cross-cultural perspective*. Yarmouth, ME: Intercultural Press.

Storti, C. (1998). *Figuring foreigners out: A practical guide*. Yarmouth, ME: Intercultural Press.

Wilson, M. S., Hoppe, M. H., & Sayles, L. R. *Managing across cultures: A learning framework*. Greensboro, NC: Center for Creative Leadership.

Background

The advice given in this guidebook is backed by CCL's research and educational experience, which dates back thirty years. For more than ten years CCL has explored leadership and management issues against the backdrop of cultural influence. During that time CCL has conducted research, published books, and led training efforts that have examined the effect of cultural difference on expatriate managers, teams, and global organizations.

CCL's research and educational work around the globe is informed by a framework that shows how leaders can learn from their cross-cultural experiences. More than a "do and don't" behavioral guide to countries outside the United States, the framework is designed to help managers see their own personal cultural lens, to recognize the cultural lenses of the people with whom they work, and to move out of a "cultural comfort zone" to establish meaningful and effective relationships across cultures.

CCL recognizes that leadership in today's multinational, multicultural business environment must be developed over time and must include an awareness of cultural influences, a flexibility with cultural differences, and an ability to communicate across cultures. Effective leaders build their capacity to work across cultures by deepening that awareness, developing that flexibility, and adjusting their communication style when dealing with people of other cultures.

Key Point Summary

Cross-cultural communication blunders can lead to serious consequences – lost confidence, lost customers, lost business relationships, and lost opportunities. Enhancing your effectiveness in communicating across cultures requires several actions. You should expect and identify cultural differences, draw cues from nonverbal communication, speak and write clearly for other cultures, learn the importance of names and titles, use humor judiciously, show your respect for other cultures, and become a lifelong learner of other cultures.

You can acquire these skills by concentrating on four points. First, examine your own cultural conditioning. Second, review your experiences with other cultures. Third, watch for discomfort that can signal cultural differences. Fourth, recognize and modify your communication approach.

The discomfort you feel when cultural boundaries collide can be used to your benefit by alerting you to cultural differences. When you feel uncomfortable, it's natural to retreat from that discomfort. To be more effective when communicating across cultures, resist that retreat. Stay with the discomforting experience and learn from it. Compare the unexpected and discomforting behaviors you experience when communicating across cultures and compare them to your knowledge of your own cultural expectations.

It's impossible to understand all the communication nuances from all the world's cultures. But in today's global business environment, if you want to present yourself as a citizen of the world and to work effectively across cultural boundaries, you must be able to communicate respect for the customs, habits, and rituals of others – especially for the people who work with you. As you become more aware of these differences and more skilled at communicating across those cultures, you become a better and more effective leader.

Ordering Information

TO GET MORE INFORMATION, TO ORDER OTHER IDEAS INTO ACTION GUIDEBOOKS, OR TO FIND OUT ABOUT BULK-ORDER DISCOUNTS, PLEASE CONTACT US BY PHONE AT 336-545-2810 OR VISIT OUR ONLINE BOOKSTORE AT WWW.CCL.ORG/GUIDEBOOKS. PREPAYMENT IS REQUIRED FOR ALL ORDERS UNDER $100.

The articles in LiA *give me insight into the various aspects of leadership and how they can be applied in my work setting.*

Clayton H. Osborne
Vice President, Human Resources
Bausch & Lomb

LiA *sparks ideas that help me better understand myself as a leader, both inside and outside the organization.*

Kenneth Harris
Claims Director
Scottsdale Insurance Company

Leadership in Action

*A publication of the
Center for Creative Leadership
and Jossey-Bass*

Leadership in Action is a bimonthly publication that aims to help practicing leaders and those who train and develop practicing leaders by providing them with insights gained in the course of CCL's educational and research activities. It also aims to provide a forum for the exchange of information and ideas between practitioners and CCL staff and associates.

To order, please contact Customer Service, Jossey-Bass, 989 Market Street, San Francisco, CA 94103-1741. Telephone: 888/378-2537; fax: 415/951-8553. See the Jossey-Bass Web site, at www.josseybass.com.